SEVEN PARTS WOMAN

Poems by Marjorie Power

SEVEN PARTS WOMAN

Poems by Marjorie Power

WordTech Editions

© 2016 by Marjorie Power

Published by WordTech Editions
P.O. Box 541106
Cincinnati, OH 45254-1106

ISBN: 9781625492012

Poetry Editor: Kevin Walzer
Business Editor: Lori Jareo

Visit us on the web at www.wordtechweb.com

Cover art: "Self Portrait with Scarf" by Brittney West

ACKNOWLEDGMENTS

Thanks to the editors of the following publications, in which these poems first appeared, some in slightly different versions.

84 Over 60: Women Poets on Love, Mayapple Press, "Looking for Frank's Obituary"

Archaeopteryx, "Shawl," "Walking Downhill in San Miguel"

Ars Medica, "Mountains that Block Sunrise"

The Atlanta Review, "Dreaming that the M.C. Is a Raven"

Blue Unicorn, "Poem Plucked in Balboa Park"

Blueline, "In the Butterfly Garden"

The California Quarterly, "Shoe Girl"

The Cape Rock, "Fear," " Kitchen Counter," " Turkish Bath"

The Dos Passos Review, "Gone Crone"

Earth's Daughters, "Slipping Away"

Eclipse, "Crow," "Designing a Necklace for Nicole," "Second Reading," "The Glove"

Edgz, "The Rocker"

Fault Lines, "Secondhand Smoke"

Hawai'i Pacific Review, "Spring Dusk, Yachats"

Main Street Rag, "My Piquantette," "Oceanfront Property"

The Malahat Review, "Humpty Dumpty, Part II"

Oasis, "The Woman the Florist Built"

Oyez Review, "Survived by Their Parents"

Parting Gifts, "December Coastline," "Deserted Beach," "Green Rope," "In the Garage," "Moon & Clock: A Local Photo," "Shaded by Sitka Spruce," "The Day Before the Fire"

Poet Lore, "In a Bruise Blue Hour"
Psychological Perspectives, "Except to Say…"
Rainbow Curve, "Preparing to Live by the Ocean"
Raven Chronicles, "Near the Parroquia"
Slant, "Broken Glass," "Her Shawl, Removed,"
    "Seven Parts Woman, One Part Art"
Third Wednesday, "Hacienda Ruin"
Trajectory, "Karen's Song"
Verseweavers, "Just After"
Voices From the Porch, Main Street Rag Publishing
    Company, "Ivy"
The Women Artists Datebook 2012, "Syracuse Cultural
    Workers"

"Why I Knit," "In a Tent" and "Waiting for a New Vocabulary" appeared in *Birds on Discovery Island,* a chapbook from Main Street Rag Publishing Company. "Palimpsest" appeared in *Faith in the Color Turquoise,* a chapbook from Pudding House Publications. "Resting on the Couch," "Still Life with Husband," "The Deaf Percussionist" and "Why Am I Unable to Ask?" appeared in *Flying on One Wing,* a chapbook from Samaritan Health Services in Corvallis, Oregon. "Sleepwalker" appeared on a poster and in a chapbook for the ReImagiNation Project in Portland, Oregon.

For my husband, Max Power, and in memory of Richard Strauss, 1937 – 1956, brother and first supporter of my writing.

Contents

I SHELL MIDDEN

On Cape Perpetua..15

Seven Parts Woman, One Part Art......................17

Preparing to Live by the Ocean.........................19

Karen's Song...20

Second Reading..21

Still Life with Husband.......................................23

Rio Caliente..24

In a Tent...26

Slipping Away...28

Mountains That Block Sunrise............................29

Humpty Dumpty, Part II.....................................30

Palimpsest...31

Why I Knit..32

The Deaf Percussionist..33

Shawl...34

II. THE WANDERER

Raven Triptych...37

Ivy..38

Turkish Bath...39

Except to Say..41

Oceanfront Property...42

Approaching Milepost 85.....................................44

The Error...45

The Day Before the Fire...46

The Glove...47

Her Shawl, Removed...49

Tuning In...51

Gone Crone..53

Green Rope...54

III. MOON & CLOCK

In a Bruise Blue Hour..57

The Rocker...58

Shaded by Sitka Spruce...59

Deserted Beach..60

Why Am I Unable to Ask?.......................................61

Moon & Clock: A Local Photo.................................62

Virtual Candles..63

Minding Our Business..65

Dreaming That the M.C. Is a Raven...........................66

Crow...67

Shoe Girl...68

Survived by Their Parents.......................................69

Designing a Necklace for Nicole...............................70

Looking for Frank's Obituary...................................71

Just After,..73

Poem Plucked in Balboa Park..................................75

IV. SPRING DUSK

In the Butterfly Garden...79

Waiting For a New Vocabulary.......................................80

Near the Parroquia..81

Hacienda Rain...82

Walking Downhill in San Miguel.....................................83

My Piquantette..86

Secondhand Smoke..87

Sleepwalker..89

In the Garage..90

Resting on the Couch..91

Spring Dusk, Yachats...92

The Woman the Florist Built..93

Fear..94

December Coastline..95

NOTES..97

BIOGRAPHICAL NOTE..99

I SHELL MIDDEN

My heart has melted into the sea.
Let it go where the waves go.

Akiko Yanagiwara

On Cape Perpetua

Wild cucumber vines
open tiny white blossoms,
let their leaves fan out.
Here's wild strawberry.
Oregon iris, also wild.

The color green crawls up and over
a mound worked by small animals.
They've left a scatter
of fragmented shells.
Green crawls beyond.

The mound is called
a *shell midden,* meaning
waste heap, summer place,
monument, memory, grave,
native inhabitant who's denied.

The horsetail fern
predates humanity.
The blackberry vine is tough too.
But neither thrives like this
clever invader, Scotch broom.

Walk with me down the trail,
across the highway and further
down, till we find a bench
among blooming sea pinks
and black lava rocks.

Let's sit by the sea.
It's playing southern today,

its waves turquoise, lazy, slack,
as if the ocean floor
couldn't possibly slip.

Seven Parts Woman, One Part Art

She had no feeling for him.
He seemed like something
by Michelangelo, a block of marble
carved to perfection. He had no feeling
for her. What they each felt for was art.

He was a sculptor of human flesh.
Her art, in his presence, seemed
not to exist. The less he knew
of who she was, the better
he could perform.

He worked on her chest
where the breast was gone.
She sat higher than he
so that her empty space
lined up at eye level for him.

He manipulated her skin
week after week, preparing it
to receive a new breast –
a synthetic object, shaped
to match, cool to the touch.

He wore the face of a soul at work.
She trusted that look, lost to all
but its focus on creation.
That gaze gave her full confidence
in his hands. She grew to accept

not liking him, not that she dis-
liked him. After his work was done

and she returned to the day,
she found her desires intact,
a flock of Harlequin Macaws.

Preparing to Live by the Ocean

The first autumn rain
gathers daylight in old woman's fingers.
Their touch penetrates me,
parched from struggling
to be rain myself.

A file of letters
heavy with whining.
Books, read long ago or never.
I will live with what words
I can carry on my back.

A shelf, empty now.
Slant afternoon sunbeams.
Dust, now you see it. Dusk,
now you don't. The phone rings.
Not someone I know. Nor am I.

A night without dreams.
A dawn without wind.
I have fewer friends
than yesterday. My heart's
a curling leaf, eager for a winter storm.

Karen's Song

Under the vast oak she croons
to three other crones
clustered in shade
whose edge creeps close
each time they settle
in their lawn chairs.

From this chosen remove
they treasure end-of-summer sun.
Through wrinkled skin
they absorb Karen's song,
a bluesy piece that floats
sadly on and on

till it becomes a shawl
that can be gathered up,
carried home and arranged
around the shoulders
in winter.

The sky quickens this
transformation, September blue
being quintessential.
When light seeps through
at this angle, it seems to hold
personal intentions.

Second Reading

Here's a detail I hadn't absorbed:
a wooden table painted green.

Another just like it
appears in chapter five
after the action moves
from farm to city.
Gambling, lust, laughter....
And towards the end of the book,
a green table. Another country now.
A different time.

The last table mentioned
is all that's left
in a cottage, after a war.
The cottage dwellers were a couple
in love. One remains alive.
High summer. Scent of hay.
Asters. Daisies. Queen Anne's Lace.

                *

The departed still come
to table, in their own way.
They appreciate a vase of wildflowers.
They want us to enjoy our meals
and one another's company.
They like us to speak of them
but only once in a while.
And not in sorrow.

As for my lifelong friend

who has fallen out of touch
for the past year and a half:
she fell in with disappointment
and unwittingly married it.
A little time lost between us
used to make no difference.
Now I wouldn't know
where to seat her, what
to serve or discuss.

Still Life with Husband

He lies on his left side, as I do. His breath begins to deepen.
Its rhythm leaves me behind, in the dark.
I try listening to the surf.

His right arm wraps me, its hand with nothing to hold.
I wonder what the absence of my breast is like for him.
I have asked, more than once, and he did answer.

I can't remember much of what he said.
When we were younger, his unfailing diplomacy
would get on my nerves.

Rio Caliente

Steam. Skin. Pulse. Breath.
This pool near the river,
buoyant with minerals.
Almost unbearably hot.

At the far end a woman speaks
of her southern California childhood.
Orange groves everywhere. Strawberry fields.
Each by each these turn to pavement.
Grown, she moves north, to the wilds of Mendocino.
Is followed by money, bringing more pavement.
Next comes Hawai'i. The Big Island. She buys a house
for herself and two to rent.... Condos rise in clumps
like mushrooms after a storm. She's thinking maybe
Central America, or an island off Spain. Warm weather's a
     must
and the sound of the ocean. Her hair:
if I painted, I'd put dune grass there.

Beside her a couple absorbs her words.
The husband begins to speak about Alaska.
His entire forty-five years. Belonging.
Home, in spite of. Silence falls
between him and the elderly wanderer.
Each offers the other a smile. He hoists his torso
from the water, hauls out one leg, now
the second. Now he grasps his cane.

As for me, I've lost a breast
and when I was eight, an older brother.
He might have won a Pulitzer, according
to my late parents. One afternoon
when they were out of earshot

he confided, *I think that you may be a born writer.* These words continue to echo in the soundless chill he left. As if he's an underground spring that provides minerals and heat.

In a Tent

My husband's breath, its rise and fall.
Sleep ushers him elsewhere.
Pines, their perfume. One by one

the stars. An autumn night so clear
the world could be anticipating a birth.
But I see lower Manhattan,

towers and bodies in flames.
Airplane wreckage. Box cutters.
The stench not mentioned in the news.

My life tumbles backwards:
I become a child, riding
to my father's place of work.

Grand Central Station. A patch of sky.
Magazine stands. The crowd. The push.
Pretzel vendors. An obscenity. A whistle.

The familiar office building. Its revolving door.
Its wooden elevator, timeless and intimate,
like a liturgical pause.

I find my father and we head uptown
to visit my great aunt, Bella,
her living room filled

by her late husband's piano.
No dust here. He always hated dust.
We're near the river. The Hudson.

When I was a child, widows lived forever.
They wore black, embroidered
with order and calm. Bella's sister,

Jeannette, became a widow and began
flying off to Europe.
After she'd return, she'd say,
I love my dirty old New York.

Slipping Away

Don't leave us, my wisp.
In your silence the world weighs more.

At three in the morning
my thoughts on a spin-dry cycle
I miss your small fingers
busy with a fountain pen.

Don't leave us, wizened peach,
smartass, wordsmith.
The media clamor
with rumors, panic, hatred.
We need your summer squall soul.
The rattle of tin cans
in your one woman parade.
The bass drum
at the heart of your poems.

Soft, soft the drumbeat.
The drummer slightly nervous.

The beach needs your footprints
and the holes from your two canes.
Who will take in four large dogs?
Stay just a little longer, my wisp.

I need the echo of you
close around me like coastal fog.
Closer than you might wish.

Mountains That Block Sunrise

A tide tugged at my husband's dreams.
I wanted to go where it pulled him.
He was ill. Needing something beyond my support,
he'd fallen for volcanic rocks
and the ocean that made them glisten.

But after we moved, the new doctor said
the one we left behind
was wrong. So the illness
was behind us too, re-diagnosed
to pose no threat.

    Now we live at the edge
of the world, at the young edge of old,
watching the old disappear.

Humpty Dumpty, Part II

After the king's horses gallop away,
Humpty's spirit, which hovers above a pile
of steaming manure, begins to jiggle
like a soft-boiled yolk.
      When he's sure
no one will hear, he tells his severed hands
to finger their way up a nearby pine. They return
sticky enough to glue back his shattered shell.
He re-attaches arms and legs,
gains purchase
on the wall, and climbs.
      Settled again
he needs a smoke.
      The June dusk takes forever.
When it's deep enough, Humpty creeps down,
toehold by toehold. He waddles through dim,
unfamiliar streets, to a store as big as a village.
If only the king's men had left him
his bottle caps....
      He grabs cigarettes
and a lighter (better than matches for rainy days).
A roll of breath mints, in case someone
approaches him from CNN or *The Times*.
Christmas ornaments, marked down –
a little glow for the pine, later on.
Finally, five or six lottery tickets.
Who cares how the dice fall?

Palimpsest

Easels. Caked palettes. The ooze of oils.
Half-finished efforts, stacked against walls.
At the artist's insistence I try to sit still.

The old stranger paints his notion of me.
I've seen what he's doing. Even at age ten
I know a woman-to-be from an ornament.

When he's done, my parents will pay him
and give me back the sky. I'll get to take off
my ironed, cornflower blue dress.

The same blue appears in this morning's dream
in clothing I wear for the painter here.
This dream studio stores emptiness. Its light

 bears nothing, no antique gold haze.
 This artist, grown old beyond telling,
 finishes me, and adds a rabbit – now,

with gusto, a hedgehog. He brushes
equal space for all, as if we were God
in three persons. Or *Alice in Wonderland*

characters, each as pivotal as the next.
Here come latitude and longitude lines
all over the enormous canvas. He begins to fuss

with details in the northwest corner.
Specks of dust, perhaps.
Atomic particles.

Why I Knit

Because a phone rings
in someone's purse.

Because I hate noise.
Because I am lost.
Lost by conversation.

Because conversation
is a layer of earth
that covers an underground stream.

Because I delight in spring
but belong to autumn. To color.
To deep and pale shades of turquoise.

I'm hopelessly in love
and want to make something of it.
A sweater, a hat, a blanket

for a newborn
whose name I embroider
in the binding.

Because I hear water
and lose track of words.
This leads to restless hands.

The Deaf Percussionist

After a woman surrenders a breast to cancer,
after she lets a doctor install an imitation,

she finds her perception of beauty
has changed. She feels akin to the blind

who see with fingers, ears, noses, and tongues.
To the deaf percussionist, who hears

through vibrations that move up her arms
and just keep going. Not to mention

the not-yet-old woman in hospice care,
at home in a rented bed,

staring out a window into flowers
she planted thirty years ago.

Her grieving family feels ready
to let her pass, but each morning

here she is. Gazing through blossoms.
At one with the flaw that bonds all sentient things.

Shawl

In a darkened sanctuary
in a loft with half a choir
women chant
in a minor key
sopranos and altos
their two parts moving
close to each other
like dancers in a slow tango
on the world's last night.

Stay with me, remain here
with me, watch and pray,
watch and pray.
Tones rise and dip,
a gift to worshippers
clumped in the first few pews.
The chant – a shawl to use
while cloth is lifted from the altar,
folded into silence
and carried elsewhere.

II. THE WANDERER

I need to recover the silence waiting
in what the body knows about time.

Frederick Zydek

Raven Triptych

All afternoon the wanderer leans against
    a moss-covered cedar and longs
for the flying raven to nest,
for the nesting raven to fly.

Three bats greet the night
    like a lost love. The raven
eyes each, and chooses.

The raven pauses at the brink of the world.
    He drops us a feather apiece.
You and I are not present.
No one is present.

Ivy

Time comes unmoored when we approach a porch
to sit side by side in its wooden swing.
Or alone, with the lurch
of a rocking chair, and a song to sing.

Sitting side by side in this wooden swing:
no one, and no one's neighbor's ghost.
There's no rocking chair or song to sing,
no wife pouring margaritas, nothing to toast.

No one, and no one's neighbor's ghost.
No hanging pots. No gardener with shears.
No wife pouring margaritas. Nothing to toast.
A green tangle holds sway, undoes the years.

No hanging pots. No gardener with shears.
Plywood, where the front door's gone.
A green tangle holds sway, undoes the years.
The giant oak's roots move under, press on.

Plywood, where the front door's gone.
A volunteer maple. A wild young ash.
The giant oak's roots move under, press on.
Lush ferns mingle with bits of trash.

A volunteer maple. A wild young ash.
There's a way through a window around the back.
Lush ferns mingle with bits of trash.
The addict. The dealer. When the sky turns black.

By morning, each has left. Come with friends
or alone, with the lurch
of your gut. Here the world begins and ends.
Time comes unmoored when we approach a porch.

Turkish Bath

I lie on a bed of smooth stone,
heated, curved for support.
Potted bamboo and coleus plants
line tile walls.
A door swings open.

A fat man appears from a steam room,
forgets to shut the door.
Such sweet scent....
Orange blossoms? Frangiapani?
I close my eyes.

To my left drift the murmurs
of an elderly couple
whose language I wish I knew.
It's more like music than words.
More like fragrance.

I have grown much older
than I thought I would
without learning the magical tongue
I'm hearing now.
It's the sun's favorite.

Strange, how a regret
that's hung on long enough
will turn inside out and glow,
a small sun to carry internally,
near the heart.

The ceiling's painted
with a sky scene –
clouds with birds.

A kind I can't identify,
an alphabet I can't read.

Except to Say...

In the warm shadows of late morning
she thinks of him.
In a foreign country, in a tiled courtyard
she remembers
certain of his words. They flit about
like butterflies.
Now a sentence alights: *Let's do this again.*
His voice joyous.
His speech more resonant in recollection,
floating against the backdrop
of a language she can't understand.
What he has given her
she cannot describe, except to say
she knew bougainvillea blooms were magenta,
coral, or red. Now she recognizes
they may also be the color of wheat.
At her age, she prefers this color
alluring only to butterflies,
that leave her to her reverie
and bless the air she breathes.

Oceanfront Property

The original house?
No one hated it. That's all I recall.
My memory goes back only
as far as the wrecking ball,
the pile of rubble.

Then came an empty spot
scraped bare, a dark flat nothing
in a rainy winter.
There were rumors.
None sparked my interest.

I envisioned a Mediterranean style villa
squeezed to the edges of the lot.
People move up here from California.
Sometimes they need to cash in,
or re-invent the sun.

For a while I was gone –
Mexico, Michigan, New Hampshire.
Gone long enough
for *lava rock* and *sneaker wave*
to slip from mind.

When I look again
I see exuberance
captured in glass.
Through clear walls,
the furniture's full of curves.

A red chair.
A yellow bench.
A table – blue.

A man and woman recline
to read.

Soon I'll move inland.
I will bring snapshots
of the home made of exuberance.
I hope to forget
those who wouldn't dream

of paying for a huge glass house.
Nor would they be caught dead
throwing stones at this one
because stone throwers,
like the very rich, don't fit in.

Approaching Milepost 85

The sky is a slightly damp
goose down comforter,
hung low, spread wide
above an auto-body shop.

Along the sidewalk, between
the row of gash/dents and the grind
of late August traffic, a neon pink jogger
drips sweat, ears plugged
with her choice of sound.

She passes a windowless
hulk of stucco. A sprawl
of parking lot. Emptiness.
The whole scene the color of dun.
Auction, still easy to read.
Listen hard and you will hear
the holler and lowing
of a prior century.

There are no more cattle.
Only packed, barren dirt,
zoning squabbles, sprayed-out
paint cans, graffiti
that's missing an artist's touch.

The Error

Many years ago I made an error.
I wouldn't say it brought no benefits.
It's come alive. Developed a stare.
Many years ago I made an error.
Sorry, I offer. *I regret you. I care.*
Sphinx-like, the gaze holds, through a pair of slits.
Many years ago I made an error.
(I wouldn't say it brought no benefits.)

The Day Before the Fire

The tan house used to be a rental.
I remember an elderly lady
kneeling in the yard. Daffodils, azaleas,
a climbing rose, daisies, dahlias, asters....
She also adored the grass.

One summer morning, she smiled
and volunteered: *I like this neighborhood
so well, I've bought my own place.*
That fall her shrubs began to tangle and blur.
The rental had been purchased by someone called Kit.

I know his name because he spoke to Phoebe once,
before he let those scraggly maples
take root, before ivy gained dominion.
Before he bought his third vehicle and parked it
straight across the path to his front door.

A second house sits squarely by the first.
A duplicate, but beige. In its garage
chaos thrives, complete with mattresses,
amplifier, drums, and a guitar
whose sound could strangle someone.

Before a universe forms, there's chaos, right?
A couch in the carport, and cigarette butts.
Stuff wadded up, stuff stacked
and lying sideways. Stained veneers
wearing through. Particle board.

The Glove

The little glove, its mitten clip.
The glove under the table.
Under the kitchen sink.
The rubber glove, sweaty inside.

The ivory kid glove tooled with flowers.
That remembers the wedding.
That wants to be a boot.
That kept its mate.

The two stored in tissue.
The brown glove, drying.
Its leather gone stiff.
The other glove.

Her oven mitt.
His surgical glove.
The cat burglar's hush.
The glove in the waste bin.

The white lace, child-sized, torn thumb glove.
The glove that made the tabloids.
The glove in the sale bin.
In the dumpster.

In the unlocked locker.
At the back of the garage.
That old baseball mitt.
The glove grown too small.

The glove still used for touchy subjects.
The fat expensive ski glove.
The ambidextrous mitten.
The parrot-like colors.

The Andes, their fingered flutes.
The cuff bracelet, the glove elbow length.
The glove, the tango, the crescent, the thigh.
The new mitten

lost outside the library.
The boxing glove, the televised fight.
The artist's model. Her hand.
The glove he paints there.

Her Shawl, Removed

Quarter note, eighth,
crescendo, breathe.
All we had to do
was give voice
and Miss Warner beamed.

In the dark, one December,
we sang outside, each
with a candle that flickered.
Snow falling. Ice underfoot.
Nobody slipped.

I was a teenager.
She was immortal.
A typical teacher, she'd never
been young, and would
never grow old.

At graduation her right arm
caught my eye.
Withered, bent,
up against her chest
in an ironed white sleeve.

How had she led us?
How did she face the world?
How did such a glaring flaw escape me?
In my plaid mind, one's right arm
was the way through life.

Winter's coming, Miss Warner, and I am lost.
 I picture you, seated in a vast white rose,
right hand nestled near your heart.

Sing to me. Please.
Sing anything.

Tuning In

My muse used to be an intellectual.
Grounded in classics, he loved long stories,
Dante's *Inferno* his favorite.
He would slip out of touch
for months, sometimes years.

Now that my hair's white
he likes to schmooze. He's an extrovert
with a parachute, glider, condo
in Aspen, pot belly
and winning smile.

I love to hear him laugh.
He isn't loud, but his voice carries
like Frank Sinatra's.
I count on hearing him sing.

His family belongs to a church
where most of my friends
wouldn't be caught dead.
I'd go if I thought he'd turn up.

He lives in an ostentatious house
whose lights shine from a hill.
Each of his five offspring
has a droid, laptop, AlphaSphere,
P.C., T.V., and studio space –
they share this – with Surround Sound.
The cacophony gladdens him. Still, he hopes
to get back to literature.

I wish he'd invite me for dinner
but his wife handles their social calendar.

She has never heard of me
and besides, we have no wavelength.

Gone Crone

An elk bone
found clean and dry.
Found hiking. Carried home.

A tall vase, empty of flowers,
washed of stems' murky residue.
A cobalt blue glass vase.

Sunbeams. A picture window.
White bed sheets
on a clothesline, snapping.

Afternoon light
spread all the way out.
An open door. Sand under-

foot. Bare, dry sand
where there used to be slime,
where a sponge once lay.

Yes, I've changed. I did warn them.

Green Rope

Tied around a Sitka spruce
the rope holds a real estate sign.
Thick twists of plastic
in a shade of green
that looks worst in winter.

The sign is metal.
Heavily rusted. A witness
to rain, shore pines,
to fog, to a highway,
to secrets held in passing cars.

The sign names two
selling agents. One is dead.
It's been a couple of years.
Since then, her widower
listed the property.

A stretch of coast walled off
from the rest of the world
by a mountain range.
Live here, and you are timeless.
Die, and you'll never be gone.

III. MOON & CLOCK

All the cows face the lower pasture.
They stare for hours at that horse,
trying to understand.

Tom Snyder

In a Bruise Blue Hour

Hot air, dead still.
Thunder's low roll.
Gunmetal gray sky detonates.
The tip of a wolf's tail
vanishes into its den
and a raven family
huddles. Each of us
freezes in the glare
of an outsized hawk.
In the river's pulse
fish continue flickering.
Don't they? There.
In the blue-black flow.
That soft glow
like opals.

The Rocker

The woman slides
gently from her sleeping husband.
She fumbles with slippers
and sleeves. Here
is the top stair.
Now the next. Here,
the switch on a small ceramic lamp.
Ice pack flexed beneath the collar
of her robe, she settles
into a rocker where
a lifetime ago
she nursed her child.
The smartest, most beautiful, etc.
Those nights, the dead lay pressed flat,
cut to size, and filed someplace.
In its covered cage
the parrot starts to rustle
against a toy bell.
Through rice paper blinds
black softens to gray.
The earliest twitter begins.
A rise in freeway roar.
Dust comes to light,
now the frame of an oil pastel.
Raise this blind, and the wild plum's
ferocious with blossoms.
That same stray cat.
Its nine lives.

Shaded by Sitka Spruce

The man.
The blueprint.
The footprint.
The dappled light.

The rafters.
The promise.
The plasterboard.
The paint.

The winter.
The crack.
The crack that re-opened.
The unreturned phone call.

The next house.
The fifth house.
The twentieth.
He built the lodge, too.

And he dreamt up a homeowners' association.
It would let him let go, move on.
He wrote pages of bylaws, handed them out.
Hired a man to keep up with the outside lights.

Deserted Beach

The ocean.
Its winter cloak
of charcoal green.
Each wave weighty,
lumbering to shore
in a white hood.

Vines creep along the ground
just above shoreline.
Wild strawberry leaves.
Tiny, but redder
than summer's fruit.
Redder than lipstick.

As red as desire
that befalls the aged,
guarded thoughtfully
so it won't need replacement
like a knee, a hip,
an artery.

Black sand.
Slick black boulders.
Wads of sea foam
mixed with a little grit –
lint left behind
by the wind.

Why Am I Unable to Ask?

Here I sit again, on the paper-covered table
in a skimpy cotton gown which I clutch
at the throat. I've already tied the thing
shut, not that it matters. The surgeon
will see to what's necessary.

If I could find something to dislike
about the man – a streak of arrogance,
perhaps, or a passion for statistics –
I'd feel more grounded. Even his Kelly green
slacks don't bother me. The color works, on him.

We women have an uneasy time.
We get biopsied for what we fear,
surrender breasts to virtual strangers.
Still, I'm grateful for the help.
I've given the surgeon

a few of my cancer poems. He says
they'll help others, and wants more.
I'm flattered, of course. But how
does he plan to use them? I still don't know
exactly what he did with my breast.

Moon & Clock: A Local Photo

Easy to imagine
what's left out of the picture,
what might lie off one edge
or another. Or above the moon.
Not that a moon this low and full
allows the eye to roam.

Mine slips anyway
across a night sky as clear as black ice
to the tower where the face
of the courthouse clock
reads five past four.

Below, on the lawn we can't see
someone may lie asleep.
Could be it's the man
with the cavernous visage

who, when I pass in daylight,
shouts: *Go to hell, ya goddamn bitch.*

Over the brightly lit clock
and under the roof line
a word is inscribed.
It might be German
which I can't read.
Or maybe a little paint
has chipped away.

Virtual Candles

Headlines bring the typical photos:
flowers, love notes, teddy bears,
heart-shaped balloons.
Survivor clings to survivor
having slipped in a pool of blood.

In an ICU a young woman
wakes up, unaware
that her child has died.
She calls and calls.
Prayers fill churches,
fly through cyberspace
with scores of virtual candles.
You can light one. Click here.

These dead are the latest offspring
of our nation's longstanding affair,
a lust masquerading as pure concern
for the protection of one's own.
If you think something's wrong
with this picture, the governor's
here to help. *This is a case of evil,*
someone who's an aberration
of nature. If it weren't one
weapon, it would be another.

Does anyone who's *not* aberrant
pull down blinds and fill his apartment
with bullets, bombs, an assault rifle
purchased with the click of a mouse?

The campaigners assure the bereaved:
none weeps alone, their grief is shared

by all of us, standing as we do
in the rockets' red glare,
hands placed over our hearts.

Minding Our Business

Next door, there's a certain dull color
on a flat-roofed, flat-faced house.
It's dullest now, while tulips bloom.

That same shade appears on storage sheds
I pass on my way to the station.
Again, down the track: Viking Fire Protection,

whose clawed V and small rippling flag
make me feel safe in some
strange new hollow of my soul.

These days, we mind our business
in a world that is ending in fire.
A world where I've developed an unlikely

penchant for institutional green.
That color pervaded my grade school.
Radiators clanked, a lifetime ago.

Bare light bulbs. Sweeping compound.
Its neon-bright particles, their brash stench.
The janitor would sweep and sweep.

Dreaming That the M.C. Is a Raven

Ladies and gentlemen, I bring you dusk.
I bring shadows as large and clumsily shaped
as your most secret hopes. I bring an unlit path
that winds all night and coils back on itself.
I bring the end of your day.
        Strangers and friends,
I bring a silken touch. I bring the caress
of a lilac-scented breeze. I bring a wind
whose direction you cannot place
and which you dare not trust,
so sweet is its draw.
        I bring the conclusion
of your resistance, ladies and gentlemen.
One at a time I will swallow you whole
and release your spirits – ghostly lunatics
awhirl in the void. At last without choice
you'll begin to love me. You'll begin
to love. You'll begin.

Crow

No one wants to eat crow.
We love stuffed turkey. Duck's a treat.
A plain-cooked chicken suffices
if it led a healthy life
running free, eating right.
Crows live on God knows what.

No one wants to hear crow.
We like listening to its cousin,
the elegant, nuanced, sophisticated raven.
And the cardinal – a heavenly voice
embodied in pure scarlet.
When a crow drops a feather
who takes it home?

Armageddon is nonsense, of course.
But let's say it's not.
Picture which, in raucous glee,
will start a world from scratch.

Shoe Girl

A shoe girl never dies.
I know one in her late eighties
who keeps her favorite stilettos
within easy reach,
just to touch them.

A shoe girl dances.
Her passion is fresh and hopeful
like Desdemona's. It's as rich and roily
as Othello's. She keeps one foot moving
just past the point of no return.

If she falls out of love, or gets bored
for other reasons, she resets her course
by glancing at the latest issue
of *Harper's Bazaar*. She also heals this way
when betrayed.

If she finds a free man who's brainy enough,
she makes a devoted mate.
My friend who sleeps
with a Life Alert button beside her stilettos
on the nightstand

remains loyal to a number of married men.
She keeps a file folder for each
including a Cuban literary agent.
Yellowed news clippings.... Those eyes....
If he were alive, I'd send him my manuscript.

Survived by Their Parents

Window by spotless window,
door by heavy door, by peephole,
brass lion, and theft protection sign,
sunrise manifests the neighbors.

Silky light finds the bare hilltop
where fresh-hewn crosses loom;
thirteen large ones, plus a small pair
for the murderous duo.

In killing themselves,
they took the rest of us hostage.
How their parents
must dread the dawn.

Two clever buddies
and their demon.
A plot, hatched quietly
in cyberspace.

A hell those two clicked on, off, on –
between haircuts, math assignments,
summer vacations, prom nights
and BMW repairs.

Designing a Necklace for Nicole

Because you have a ballerina's neck.
Because you're grown, about to graduate.

Because of the massacre
at the high school close to yours.

Your town pours into a field
to lay flowers there.

My mother and your grandmother
grew up together.

They knew Saturday nights
by gun fights at the saloon.

Their West preceded Hollywood's.
Yours virtually follows.

Because of your dancing.
Because I have no daughters.

Because my mother has passed away
leaving these amethysts and pearls.

A teacher bled to death.
They were all looking forward.

Because the killers were about to graduate.
Because the killers killed themselves.

Because my mother was spared this news
your grandmother hears.

Looking for Frank's Obituary

On drizzly afternoons
when nobody's here
and the parrot snoozes
I sometimes go online
to see whether Frank has died.

I type his full name
and the word *obituary*
in the search box.
Now his city and state.

Here are journals
that include Frank's work,
none of them recent.
Now a website
for heartland playwrights.
Word of his visits
to an abbey in Wisconsin.
A photo, new to the internet,
taken on the campus
where he taught for thirty-five years.
Here's his first name
cached among others,
his last attached to a Robert
who lives in Oakland.
Now a complete poem

by none other than Frank.
I wish we could still be friends.

I want to forgive him.
I don't know why
he needs to be dead first.

I could pay for a web search....
Maybe I'll try googling his alias,
the name he uses for blue movie scripts.
If that guy has an obituary,
it's possible Frank's gone too.

I do not know which to prefer.../
The blackbird whistling/Or just after.

Wallace Stevens

Just After,

as in: A song-shaped hollow.
A very brief coda
composed by a bird.
A silence that follows
conversation in which love
remains undisclosed.
Breath sucked in and held
after a late autumn branch
lets its last leaves go.
The startle of integrity
revealed through what's bare,
gnarly, idiosyncratic, crooked
or grayish brown.
The carol about the rose
that blooms in winter. Both
the notes and the words.

A wisp of early morning fog floats down a mountain
to wrap an old woman and cushion her from those who
knock at the door, invite her out, insist she sail with them
through the lifting day to see a butterfly collection – two
large cases of Swallowtails, Skippers, Monarchs of course,
and most exquisite of all, the Morphos. Who'd think a
creature named for death would shimmer with electric blue
light? On her front porch, the old woman shifts her feet.
Offers regrets. Turns away. Gazes into the living room
toward last week's unexpected gift – parcel wrap neatly

folded into a tiny boat. She steps into the house, brushing
past a rarely pruned tangle that occupies the door frame.

A jolt of joy
at a chrysalis glimpsed
suddenly and from the side.

Poem Plucked in Balboa Park

A whirl of blossoms.
Sculpted shrubs. A fountain.

Invisible gardeners bend, manipulate,
rise, move on, and bend, working each swatch of lawn back
to the Elysian fields. November's a perfect balance
of shadow and sun. A steep light, but still warm.
Sit down with me

please, near these onion domes,
their black and blue tiles circling
with white and gold. Let's be,
for a moment, where the quarter hour chimes.
My gnarled old mother would have read
all morning here, sometimes glancing up
to face her grief. Her secret grief which had at last
quit its bruising ways.

IV. SPRING DUSK

I will be kind to bilious men
for whom the boulevard
is just a tarry smear
of gloom. I'll give them room….

Jean Esteve

In the Butterfly Garden

If Eve's error-of-choice
began with a fig tree,
as Biblical scholars
surmise, hers must not
have been *a strangulated fig,*
our guide's appellation for
this greedy looking growth
which happens to be doing the strangling.

*

What gets lost in translation
turns to fuzz, grows legs.
A baby tarantula crawls forth.

*

If heaven is blue
its color was scraped
from the wings
of butterflies such as these
by an envious angel.

*

Our guide steps close to observe
a butterfly folding shut.
Speckled brown camouflage
whose largest spot looks like an eye
from a tiny owl. This genus is called
Morpho, she purrs, rolling the "r" – as if
in this sprawling screen tent
death were a succulent fruit.

Waiting For a New Vocabulary

We raise blinds to late autumn dawn.
This room, its walls of "Peach Smoothie."

This room. The color
of joy, chosen
when I painted this house.

Bare branches. A void
where branches sway.

A vast black gash in the world,
two months fresh. A morning
that unveiled the year's deepest blue
set ablaze, cremated,
stolen from time.

By our bed, my slippers.
One with a drip of paint.

Near the Parroquia

Like an aimed object, the old woman
takes on a stretch of cobblestones
whose mortar has washed away
beneath vehicles, vendors, small children,
mothers, businessmen,
beggars, tourists
and dogs.
    Along the walled street
past a row of elaborate doors
she moves as if weightless
beneath a dark woolen shawl.
Her face a broken clay pot
glued together, a riverbed gone dry.
An arrowhead no one will collect
so swiftly does she fly.

Hacienda Ruin
for Max

A gate would keep us
off these grounds
but the gate is gone.
We step under the arch
toward what's left of the home.
Even the graffiti looks centuries old
faded by high desert sun.

Doors would require us
to knock, to state our purpose.
The doors – stolen, dragged
lurchingly away by starlight,
each with its large brass knocker
and elaborate carvings.

The thieves would have walked in silence,
mesquite branches clawing their legs,
sharp stones almost causing them to trip.
They would have embodied patience,
born knowing that dust returns to dust.

Everything left is falling down.
Ceilings, walls, mortar, bricks
crumble and fall into nopal and prickly pear.

A blue day, acacia in bloom,
a yellow blaze everywhere we turn.
Let's stay here, just the two of us
and shadows that come with evening.
No medical conditions
whose strange names
we never imagined we'd learn.

Walking Downhill in San Miguel

Like squared-off, gargantuan, grounded
balloons, new houses cluster on the hilltop.

Tile roofs, walls painted various clay shades
to match the old city down slope. As if

the almost six hundred years of *historia,
tradicion y valor* belonged to the view.

Red and magenta flare from bougainvillea vines.
Signs read Casa McHugh, Casa Roy Smith.

Here's a small mural of Guadalupe. (Word is
Mexicans own a few of these homes.)

Lacy metal flower boxes overflow with leaves –
but this one's filled with wads of plastic bags.

Now Styrofoam, a condom, cigarette butts.
Near one front door, now another, *se vende* signs.

Also for sale, a bare lot. *Se vende* fading. Trash rising.
Sidewalk smooth as the day it was poured.

Smooth as unquestioned faith in real estate sales.
Poured for those ready to acquire a view of a world

　　*

that walks on cobblestones.
Map open, my husband stands
half a block ahead of me.
Says there's a pedestrian path
coming up to our left.

Not that this street
could accommodate a car.
A motorcycle, yes.
Or a pair of burros.

Now we are looking
left and down

toward the beginning
of time. My love
folds his map,
sets foot on stair one.
I must not look
at the beginning of time.
I must look where I must step.

Stair one pitches forward.
Stair two tilts right.
Stair three is useless.
Stair four has a rail to grasp.
Stair nine: no more rail.
Stair fifteen's deep,
providing respite.
Stair twenty-six
marks the halfway point.
Surely we've gone halfway.

  *

A soul enveloped in a black shawl steps off the long street
into the vast cavern of an empty church. Perhaps she will

light a votive. Perhaps she'll simply genuflect and kneel,
facing the blue-clad Virgin in her halo of golden spikes

or the thorn-crowned Christ. We pass the church, turn
another corner. A sky-blue house, a pink door, a sudden

boy. *Hola!* he declares, beaming with his whole being. Just
three more blocks of small dwellings and shops, and we'll

reach the casita. Another wall, and behind it, Casa Jesus,
Casa Diaz.... Guadalupe again, faded here, lush plants

at her feet, arch overhead with a light bulb for evening.

My Piquantette

She is the niece
of Mother Goose
with whom she studied voice
and in whom she confides love secrets.

She's a full-throated chuckler,
pink-caned warbler,
elder with fork-ed tongue.

My piquantette is a card-carrying genius.
She sheds thoughts
the way a molting parrot
drops feathers – the long and the strong,
the bits of downy fluff
she dismisses like dust bunnies.
Occasionally I pick up a flight feather.
I'd like to collect these
but they're easy to lose.

I manage to keep a paper scrap
with the signature of my piquantette.

In her flowerpot hat
and cotton gloves
she's as dainty as a doll
on a wedding cake.

Secondhand Smoke

Your match flares.
The others you invited to lunch

tip the waitress and rise,
a small flock of polite excuses:
a seventy-something gambler
who quits while he's ahead,
his shiny headed friend
who exudes empathy around the table,
a skinny seventeen year old blue eyed Buddhist
who helped you drive all the way out here to the coast.
Now an elderly soul who *used to teach*
with Stanley Kunitz, back when Bennington
was a force to reckon with.

Bobby lingers, leaves his sweet touch on my shoulder.

Your cigarette glows: we're alone,
chimichanga plates removed.
Among plastic snapdragons
and canned Mexican songs.
Beneath glass chilis
and parrots that repeat nothing.
You lean closer, lower your voice.

Bobby lived for a while in a cabin
maybe twenty miles east of Portland.
In those days, he was Madame Chang.
Madame Chang wore silk dresses
slit up the side, and a wig
with chopsticks. She played piano
every night in a Portland bar.
This next part is where Jeff comes in.

He and Bobby just celebrated their fortieth.
Jeff enjoyed that bar. It was posh.
He hadn't seen the likes of it in Little Rock.
Jeff fell in love with Madame Chang!
He'd never heard such music,
never seen such a woman.

Sleepwalker

Mid-stride, mid-morning
the sleepwalker opens his eyes.
He's as naked as Adam.

What garden is this? Why
all these snails – outsized, airborne?
How can a rainbow hang in strings

that blow in the breeze
and flow along his limbs,
that connect with snails,

leaf-laden boughs, whatever lives?
He shuts his eyes again to focus
on the tingle and warmth of his skin.

He knows everything here has already
received its name, and if he listens,
he will learn his own.

In the Garage

Big, like a football player.
He's here for my donation
to the Children's Home,
an elliptical trainer he hefts
into the bed of his pickup.

His hand clasps mine,
the shake an engulfment.
His name's the same
as my brother's,
the one killed
when I was a child.
A name lodged
between heart and gut.

His handshake stops time.
It's a lifting-out-of,
placing me in a world
where my brother moves,
AIDS has died off,
and there's silence
in the Gaza Strip, broken
by birdsong.

Resting on the Couch

She lies entirely
on the left side of my chest,
little pink legs tucked up,
head turned sideways.
Fashionistas covet hair like hers,
flaming red tufts
that catch the light
and point everywhere.

She dozes comfortably
atop my reconstructed breast.
I've begun thinking of it
as an art purchase
that's wearing well.

Such quick, determined breathing.
My granddaughter!
I with no sister,
niece, female cousin
or daughter of my own.

Spring Dusk, Yachats

The salal blooms —
pale pink droplets on red stems.
Its leaves go gray with fungus.
My cousin, too, is uniquely
beautiful and unhappy.

If you love someone
who has everything
but still sounds hollow,
after sunset listen only to the ocean.
Gather shadows.

Try a narrow path
used by rabbits and deer.
Disappear among shore pines
and Sitka spruce. Be your absence.
Be present to that.

Return to the beach
where the ocean grows dark
and the tide delivers your name.
Where the hollow might stroll
and the new moon rises.

Along the rocky trail,
a blast of fragrance
offered by wild roses
while their cultivated sisters
sleep, snug in green's dark core.

The Woman the Florist Built

Imagining an enormous doll
the florist works a wire frame, for fall
winds to pass through, and winter's chill.

Her figure takes shape. He adds flowers and moss
that go brown with sun, stiff with frost.
She weathers gusts of rain while leaves toss

and the throng of passers-by dwindles.
Her admirers, home now, kindle
dreams. Cold light twists around a spindle,

thread for a fabric the homeless wear.
Tonight, outside the florist's door,
a man recalls his first love.

Fear

To fear is to stand
at a bedroom window
early in the morning
and hesitate
to raise the blind.

Once it's up
you see February sky
that begins to show color.
The sparkle of branches,
roof tops, fence posts.
Winter heather,
purplish pink blooms
grown plump.
A cloud of a cat

models perfect indifference
and still, you can't
welcome the view.

To fear is to fail
to confide in a friend
when any would offer support.

It's to stand at a window
and watch snow melt,
then go on watching.

December Coastline

A Christmas card arrives,
deer in a quiet glade.
Near my own home, the tide
drags in, each wave elephantine.
Hunks of foam fly.

It's raining sideways.
The roar of the wind
is the roar of the surf
is the aria of December
on the Oregon coast.

In trees, tufts of Spanish moss blow
like beards of little old wild men.
There's something
I wanted to tell you.
The wind must have taken it.

NOTES

The four epigraphs are from poetry collections. The first, by Akiko Yanagiwara, who wrote under the name "White Lotus," is from a poem with no title in *Three Women Poets of Modern Japan*, trans. Glenn Hughes and Yozan T. Iwasaki. The second is from "Walking Naked Through the Woods," *At the Edge of the Ancient Inland Sea*, Frederick Zydek. The third is from "Cow Quartet," *Two Dogs and a Cigar*, Tom Snyder. The fourth is from "I Will Be Kind," *The Winter Sun*, Jean Esteve.

Many of these poems were seeded by my life on the central Oregon coast. I moved there in late 2004 and stayed three years.

"Rio Caliente" was written in 2007 after spending eight days at a rustic resort by that name, in the mountains outside the city of Guadalajara in Mexico. The resort, established by a doctor in the 1920's, was named after a river that flows through the property.

"Ivy" was written after a trip to Detroit in the summer of 2012.

"In the Butterfly Garden" was inspired by a half day's visit, in the winter of 2000, to Carara National Park in Costa Rica.

"Near the Parroquia," "Hacienda Ruin" and "Walking Downhill in San Miguel" were written during and after my second trip, in the winter of 2012, to central Mexico.

BIOGRAPHICAL NOTE

Marjorie Power grew up in Stamford, Connecticut and graduated in 1969 from San Francisco State College (now, San Francisco State University). She spent most of her adult life in Washington and Oregon, and moved to Denver, Colorado in 2015.

Her poetry appears in six chapbooks and one full length collection, all from small presses: *Faith in the Color Turquoise,* Pudding House; *The Complete Tishku,* Lone Willow Press; *Birds on Discovery Island,* Main Street Rag Publishing Company; and others. Over 400 of her poems have been published in journals and anthologies, some of which are listed on the Acknowledgments page of this collection. She enjoys reading her work aloud and has given many readings.

Marjorie and her husband, Max, enjoy dancing, hiking, attending the theater, travel, and family time. They have six grandchildren.

Made in the USA
San Bernardino, CA
25 September 2016